THE
ART OF
ADVOCACY

The Ten Commandments of
Defending Criminal Cases

By

Robert Ansell

Silver Wolf Press
PO Box 271, Cooper Station
New York NY 10276
www.silverwolfpress.com
info@silverwolfpress.com

Original Edition ©2005 Robert Ansell
Cover Design: Gigi Cavanaugh

ISBN#: 0-615-12971-4
Barcode#: 978-0-615-12971-6

<u>DEDICATION</u>

To my father, Leon, with thanks for my genes.

To my wife, Gabrielle, with thanks for my jeans.

To Sofia, Luke and all of my children.

Special thanks to Brian Ansell for his feedback, research and support.

TABLE OF CONTENTS

PREFACE

This is a postcard from the end of the road; my travels in the law were completed some time ago. It's not a Wish-You-Were-Here postcard. I had a great time on the journey, but I'm not recommending it for anyone else. I'm not knocking it either. I just think it takes a special person to try criminal cases for a living. A glutton for punishment, actually. Aside from the system stacked against you, if you are successful, you are in court all day, leaving only nights and weekends for the rest of the work – the mail, phone calls, research, dictation, appointments, preparation, etc. And always subject to the power of judges, a group that now bears more of a resemblance to Henry Ford than John Marshall. I never looked at it that way before I signed on.

On the other hand, I do tend to romanticize the work. All professions have their *glitterati*. In medicine, it's the surgeons. In football, the quarterback. In the military, the fighter pilots and in music, the guitar player. I like to think of litigators as the "white scarf" folks of the law.

The phenomenon of trying cases is supposed to be an advancement in the process of "civilization." They keep

7

telling us that the quantum leap in resolving societal disputes was when we moved to trial by word instead of trial by deed – you know, the hot knife on the tongue, the gauntlet, dunking.

Since you are reading this, you're probably in law school.[1] After you've actually tried a case or two, you'll probably think you have nothing to learn from anyone. Actually, I don't really have anything to teach you; just some things to remind you of. After all, like most things in life, trying criminal cases is just common sense.

Also, there is probably nothing in here that can **really** prepare you for the profession you are entering. Nor can anything else. You can moot-court this and you can moot-court that, but nothing really prepares you for the sense of awe and responsibility that accompanies your first experiences. I majored in Estate Planning and Trusts in law school. I was so scared in my first trial (non-jury, Municipal Court) that I could hardly speak. Fortunately, Judge Jones[2] was a friend of my father (also a

---

[1] Or you love *CSI* and *Law and Order*.

[2] There are a lot of different people named Jones in here. They are not related. In fact, they are not even Jones.

lawyer) and he told the defendant from the bench that he was giving him a light fine because his lawyer didn't waste the court's time with a lot of useless argument.

But there are a few war stories in here that you might relate to. My small-town practice brought me some interesting cases and experiences, as well as the benefit of time. A lot of time. I'm old. When I clerked for an Appellate Court after law school, I worked on a copyright infringement case involving the **wet** photocopy machines. In fact, I was around when the secretaries would ask, "How many carbons?" That might make me a dinosaur, but the core precepts of trying cases really don't change much over time.

Or context, for that matter. The craft is the craft. Criminal law is just the context. I told this to my partners once and their response was to send me when a mortgage foreclosure found its way into court. Frankly, I knew zilch about mortgages, but my adversary, a very distinguished real estate attorney, knew diddly-squat about being in a courtroom. We settled. Fortunately, I never had to try a matrimonial case. The closest I came was in the breakup of a pediatric medical practice when I watched the two doctors fight over custody of a scale.

I can offer you this advice -- develop a store load of patience. You are entering a system with a skewed view of time. This system will assemble 75 lawyers to a calendar call, and keep them glued to the courthouse for 2 or 3 days so a single judge will not have to wait 1 hour to start a case. This was hard for someone as impatient as me. It was before cell phones. Before fax machines. Sitting in a lounge for endless hours. Going over the same file. Over time, I became engaged to a phone booth in the lower corridor. In a civil case, this affected both sides. In a criminal case, of course, it affected only defense lawyers. The Prosecutors' offices were in the courthouse building. They were home. I'm sure it's all different now. I hope so.

I decided to use mostly my own cases to illustrate the COMMANDMENTS because –

1. I am an egomaniac;

2. It's what I know from direct experience;

3. All of the above.

I do not often use cases I lost because:

1. I am an egomaniac;

2. There were none;

3. I don't want to be sued for malpractice;

4. Two of the above.

Hyperbole being the default province of anyone writing the ten commandments of anything, I may hammer a thing or two to make a point. But, basically, this is what I know and this is how I learned it. Frankly, I think I'm better at exposition than story-telling, but I hope that the "this is how I learned it" sections will make it all the more real and fun for you. They did for me, both in the living and writing of them.

In the end, I feel like Chauncey in Kozinski's *Being There* – everything I know in life I learned, well, not from gardening, but from defending criminal cases.

FIRST COMMANDMENT

GET YOUR MONEY UP FRONT

Money in the law works just as it does everywhere else; it defines value. The more they pay you, the more they think you're worth. Setting fees is an art, of course. It's not that difficult. There is a market that sets value and you will plug into that. But, collecting them is just as important as setting them.

Don't kid yourself. You're not dealing with the crème de la crème here. This is not a cultural cross-sample. Most of the potential or real defendants that are sitting in front of you are looking for ways to beat you just as they looked for ways to beat the system that brought them to be sitting in front of you. And usually they are sitting in front of you in trouble, angry, scared. It all amounts to a lot of tension. I'm glad I got to experience the other end of this spectrum. During my first two years in law school, I worked in a tuxedo-rental store. Every one who came in was going to a wedding, bar-mitzvah, graduation, anniversary party. They were all happy, secure, looking forward with great anticipation. Not your clients.

Remember that in most jurisdictions, once you file

your Appearance in a criminal case, you are on the hook and will find it difficult to be relieved as counsel, especially for financial reasons. Judges, who are under tremendous pressure to move their caseloads, will not treat you kindly, especially when they are asked to protect a fee to you that might amount to a good portion of their yearly recompense.

So, if you're going to be on the hook anyway, might as well make sure you're covered. Once the case ends, your clients will have no interest whatsoever in paying you. If you win, they say they were innocent anyway and didn't really need you. If you lose, they say they could have done that by themselves and saved a lot of money in the process.

This doesn't mean that you shouldn't work for free. Nothing wrong with that. Aside from making a contribution, you might find, as I did, that some of your most interesting work comes in the pro bono area. The point is to make it your choice when you work for pay and when you don't. Don't let the client choose for you.

And, by the way, retainer collecting can be fun,

running the gamut from the alleged "paperhanger"[3] reaching into his wallet to write a check (I told him to take it across the street to the bank, cash it and bring me the proceeds) to the alleged heroin pusher who screamed his innocence while paying my $5000 retainer in 10's and 20's.

Also, keep in mind that many clients who scream poverty seem to find the funds to take matters in their own hands if they think they can beat the system. I had a bookmaker come to my office after the adjournment of his first trial date to tell me that I should congratulate him for getting the delay. He had been approached by an associate who said that for $1000, he would guarantee the adjournment through nefarious means that involved his brother-in-law and the high-school, best friend of a sister of a judge's hairdresser. Or something like that. Guaranteed. No adjournment, no payment. He had paid the money and was delighted by the adjournment. I was just as delighted to tell him that he had been ripped off. Almost every case was adjourned at its first trial date, and this guy's associate was just scoring on the inevitable. Some of these people will amaze you. They'd much to

---

[3] Someone who passes bad checks

prefer to pay ten times as much to do something illegitimately.

I've been beaten by some of the best (and worst) of them, but less often as time went on. I also spent some time in the wow-this-is-fun-I-can't-believe-they-pay-me for-this mode. But, the money is important, not only because it pays the bills. It is also a metaphor for the value of what you do, not only to your client, but also to yourself.

By the way, you've heard the old joke about the three most often-told lies. Well, the fourth is "I'll get you your retainer **after** you get me out on bail." [4]

And then, of course, there are some times when money just doesn't matter. You will be reading about some cases in the following pages that simply could not have been turned down, no matter what the finances. They were opportunities to kick ass. Never turn down an opportunity to kick ass. They don't come that often.

---

[4] Remember, when you go to see a client or prospect in jail, bring a lot of business cards.

SECOND COMMANDMENT

KEEP IT SIMPLE

Trials are not that difficult. It's just like the old saw. There is the Opening Statement, when you tell the jury what you are going to do. There is the Testimony, when you do it. There is the Closing Statement, when you tell the jury you did it.

And, during all of this, you might look at the time that is passing as *good*, *neutral*, or *bad*. *Good time* is when you are making progress, either on the issues of the case, the wonderfulness of the defendant or the beauty of your tie or scarf. *Neutral time* is usually OK for you (under the ancient Latin theorem – "it ain't bad"), but be careful not to allow so much that you bore or distract the jury, unless, of course, you want the jury bored and/or distracted. *Bad time* is your enemy. The helpfulness of this perspective is in inverse proportion to its simplicity. If what is happening in the courtroom is good for you, keep it going. If not, do what you can to stop it. The idea, of course, is to have as much *good time* as possible. There's a concept.

Before you do anything, there is the process of jury

selection. Here's where you start to get real simple. The only inviolable rule I followed was to look for jurors I could relate to and who could relate to me. I focused on that quality as crucial to anything I might want to do. Sometimes I wanted an intelligent jury. Sometimes one not so intelligent. Sometimes cohesive, sometimes fragmented. The variables are innumerable, but, at bottom, I had to be able to reach them, to make contact.

The verdict doesn't always tell you whether you were right or wrong in the selection process. The case might just have been an automatic winner or loser. And, you never know what really goes on in that jury room, no matter how long you try cases. In New Jersey, it was unlawful to speak to jurors after the verdict, so I was deprived of direct feedback. But once, in what was known as a "big" murder case (as if any murder case could be small), the six-month length of the trial created an amazing bond among the jurors and they held a reunion one year after the verdict and invited the lawyers. Fascinating. These were people I had seen every day for six months, but had never spoken to. What would be going on in their minds after such a tense, intellectually-draining experience? Which of my brilliant thrusts of strategy and rhetoric would they focus on? The first thing that happened when I walked in the door of the restaurant was Juror #2 coming up to me, reaching out and straightening out the knot in my tie. "I've been wanting to do that every day for six months," he said.

I forgot this COMMANDMENT and decided to get fancy once. It was a mercy killing case. A young man had been paralyzed from the neck down in a motorcycle accident and over the following three days in the Intensive Care Unit, he begged his younger brother to kill him and his wife not to interfere. As he so tragically put it, he could not bear to spend the rest of his life as "a head on a bed." The younger brother obliged him by bringing a sawed-off shotgun into the ICU and shooting him. The charge was Murder-One. The defense was temporary insanity.

Obviously, the case was extremely charged emotionally and brought religious considerations into the courtroom in what I was afraid could be a devastating way. I wanted jurors whose main attribute was open-mindedness. Not so easy in the rural, conservative community in which the case would be tried. I had heard that in one of the early Berrigan trials, the defense team conducted an attitudinal survey of the pool from which the jurors would be selected. We didn't have much money, so, after retaining a forensic psychologist new to this field to draft the survey, I hired some high school students to do the telephone and collation work. Jurors were taken from the Registered Voter's List, so we surveyed a sample of the registered voters of the county.

After all of the processing and collating (by hand; no computers then), the results of the survey were quite clear. My ideal juror was a young, black, gay, Jewish, professional Democrat – with children. I don't know how many of them there were on the planet at that time, but none found their way to my jury.

But, this case was also the first and only time I tried to investigate the actual potential jurors, instead of just a representative sample. A couple of weeks before the trial, we could obtain a list of the group of three hundred registered voters from which the actual jury would be drawn (Amazing. Very few lawyers knew this.). We were not allowed to contact the candidates, of course, but I saw no reason why we could not drive by their houses. This is where it got real important to get simple, so that the results were uniform and readily accessible. The high school kids and I had a ball with this, first debating what to look for in a "drive-by". We settled on such things as pets, American flags, make of car, bumper stickers, laundry on the clothes line (it was the early '70's), neatness, financial level, openness. It was a lot of fun and a lot of work and it saved me at the trial from accepting a candidate who looked really good on paper, but whose "drive-by" card showed 2 American flags, intense chain link fencing and a John Birch Society bumper sticker.

Putting grandiose experiments aside, picking a jury is common sense, really simple and it's best to keep it that way. There are the rules, of course, and you probably have been taught most of them. And, we all develop our little preferences along the way. Pay attention to them if they work for you. I liked pinky rings on men, and full lips on anyone. I used to try cases against an Assistant Attorney General who always looked at the heels on the shoes of the prospective jurors as they passed on their way into the box. Heels? He would never tell me why. I guess he didn't want to give up his edge, or lift, as it were.

At the end of the day, jury selection is often the most important part of the trial process. In terms of result, many cases are over at this point. All of your preparation, oratorical genius and tactical brilliance will mean precious little if you are defending an armed robber in front of twelve *7/11* night clerks. You know what I'm saying?

The Opening Statement is the first of only two opportunities to address the jury directly. Until the summation, you will be speaking to them through witnesses (and, if you're clever, through your dialogs with the judge that aren't at side-bar). It's your chance to make a relationship with the jury, outline your case and, most importantly, anticipate the problems so you can begin to work on the jury's mind set with respect to them. This is crucial. Only let them be surprised by what you want them to be surprised by. You have to exert control over the flow of information to them. If you control the information, favorable or adverse, then you control the timing of its release. If you don't control the information and it is adverse, better to spring than be sprung.[5]

---

[5] Don't forget. The most important choke-point of the **pre**-trial information flow lies in the throats of your clients. Keep them quiet. They rarely help themselves, with the cops, the press, witnesses, friends or anyone else. Tell them to blame you for their refusal to discuss the case with anyone who asks. It gets them off the hook.

And, as a general rule, you have to find a way to relax, be comfortable and natural in what you are doing so the jury can feel the same way. No matter how many times you've done it. You need to get comfortable in this courtroom, in this time, in this set of circumstances. Early on in your career, you might want to open your Opening with a stock piece of material (a paean to the wonderfulness of jury duty, for example) – something you can lean back against as you settle in.

In one of my first, big, "national" trials, I was nervous as I stood to address the jury on Opening on a cold winter New Jersey day. As I began to speak, I realized that the static electricity in my socks had prevented my pants legs from sliding down when I rose. I looked like George Washington (fortunately, there was no Court TV in those days) and spent the next few minutes alternatively shaking my legs like I was in shock therapy, all the while trying to pretend that nothing unusual was going on. Had I been comfortable at the time, I would have simply leaned over and taken care of the situation. Of course, my co-counsel never let me forget this. They referred to me as "Mr. President" for the rest of the trial. It was a long trial.

On **Direct Examination**, assuming you have any

case at all, the usual concern is order of presentation of witnesses and the order of the internal testimony of each. Don't lose sight of the need to keep it interesting. The jurors are an audience. Treat them like one. Humor works. When all else fails, do or say something funny. Just make sure it's funny.

Cross Examination is generally your battlefield. You will be doing a lot of tearing down. In the courtroom, someone is usually building up and someone is tearing down. Tearing down is your lot. Most often, you won't have anything to build with.

Cross is not that complicated. You always have three choices – use, refuse or abuse.

Use – Even in the worst of circumstances, there's almost always something you can get that helps you, something that can give you *good time*, even if it's just the fact that the proof of your client's innocence is that he didn't attempt to flee at the time of the arrest (even though he may have been surrounded at the time by fourteen SWAT teams). You are in control. You are the one who decides which subject matters are open for discussion and which are not. It really is simple. If you want to talk about the weather, ask a question about the weather.

If not, don't. The witness cannot talk about the weather (or, more to the point, anything adverse to your interests) if you do not ask about the weather.

I once saw a colleague get forty-five minutes of *good time* in the cross of a most hostile investigating police officer by focusing his entire cross-examination on the one sentence in the thirty-page Police Report where the defendant said he was concerned for his family: that allowed my colleague to delve into details of the family, including names, nicknames, ages, schooling, sports and activities of all the children; demeanor of the defendant; situation of the defendant – here he is, in trouble, in jail, and all he can do is muster concern for his family, and so forth, and so on.

Refuse – You may get paid by the hour, but rarely by the word, so don't hesitate to forego cross if it's clear that you can make no use whatsoever of the witness. I had to do that many times, the most painful of which was in a murder case. In my home jurisdiction, we had a Coroner who thought he was a cop, rather than an independent resource that had no vested interest in the outcome of a case. It was a single-shot homicide and, at the Preliminary Hearing, the Coroner testified that the bullet retrieved from the body at the autopsy had been "notched"; that is, an indentation had been filed in the slug. This would make the bullet explode upon impact and greatly increase the damage it could cause. Filing the tip of the slug was extremely telling evidence of premeditation, evidence that would put my client in line for Murder-One. This testimony at the Preliminary Hearing was used by the Prosecutor to have bail set at an enormously high amount.

The autopsy revealed the path of the bullet, the damage it caused and one small anomaly – a 1/4 inch piece of metal about the width of a paper clip that was found in the abdominal cavity. After looking at the inventory of the deceased's clothing in the Police Report, we found the she had been wearing a corset at the time of the shooting. It was quite obvious that the bullet had hit one of the little corset hooks on the way in and that was what had caused the bullet to "notch" and that was what explained the little piece of metal found in the body cavity.

So, at the subsequent trial, you can imagine how stoked I was for my cross-examination of the Coroner, armed with his sworn testimony at the Preliminary Hearing and ready to pounce. To tell the truth, I never liked him anyway. I'm not sure I can explain how difficult it was to refrain from laying this guy out. But the case turned on another issue (who fired the shot) and it would have been totally gratuitous of me to quench my blood lust by beating up on him. I would have also risked turning off the jury.

"No questions, Your Honor," when it came to be my turn.

That was hard, but effective. It's really no different than any other arena. I am a musician now, and the most important thing I have learned here is that the notes I don't play are as important as the notes I do. Put another way, the space you leave is as important as the space you take.

There is a "psychology" to cross. It's really all about attitude. And the basic, underlying attitude always is: I am in control. I am going to ask you about the things I want to ask you about. You will answer my questions. You will not make speeches. I am in control. I will not be hurt by you. Attitude!

Abuse – If you are inexperienced and/or insecure, you may feel the need to put on a show for your client – to justify your fee or meet your client's expectations or demands ("Gimme some action for all that money I paid you.") This is a trap. Abuse is your last resort. Never, ever, attack a witness unless you have to. It's not nice and it doesn't work.

If you must, then the point, of course, is to be successful, even if that means limiting the attack to a very small area. Most of what you need to know when in attack mode is subsumed in the COMMANDMENTS that follow. But, specifically, you might want to pay attention to the following:

1. Before you start, ask yourself the question: Am I better off if I don't try, or if I try and fail?

2. Know your style, the one that works for you, that gives you a voice and perspective. Are you a scalpel, a chisel, a chainsaw?

3. Look for the escape routes in any subject matter you are going to probe and close them – close them quickly(so it's over), close them out of context(so they do not look like escape routes), close them gently(so you get what you want from the witness before things get hostile).

4. Try to find that place and rhythm where the witness almost disappears; where it's about the questions, not the answers; where the answers are quick blips and the questions become a stream of communication to the jury, communication of your position. *Good time*. Delicious!

The Closing Statement – The first thing to deal with (this applies to The Opening Statement as well), is to figure out how you are going to work when you address the jury. 1. How are you going to communicate with the jury? 2. How are you going to communicate with yourself while you communicate with the jury?

1. Are you going to read your statement word for word, or present it as-you-go from some materials or the total unknown. Reading is certainly not recommended; it's difficult enough to keep the jury awake. But if you must, at first, do it. In the choice of getting good material out poorly, or bad material out well, I choose the former.

But it's best that you find some way to present the material more spontaneously. I always used an outline – it's the closest thing to the way my mind works – all issues and sub-issues, indentations, intense tabbing. Most lawyers I worked with and against used notes – reminders, quotes, comments too good to leave to chance. If you come up with a good line in the shower that day, write it down so you get it right. A good line "brands" your position. I'll never forget listening to my brother, Richard, sum up to a jury in a civil, wrongful-death action (on behalf of a plaintiff whose son was killed) against a slum lord whose tenement burned to the ground: "The defendant wanted to make a killing in real estate. He did!" Something like "If it doesn't fit....". It's a helluva thing when a Summation line burns itself into the consciousness of a culture.

2. I used a yellow pad. Some used index cards, paper napkins, and now a computer screen. This is important. It should not be a happenstance. Think about it. What works for you? Can you continue to make it better? It's all about comfort and retrievability.

As for the content of your remarks, well, you'll figure this out. Pay attention to the "stock" material. There are certain things you will be talking about in Summation in almost every case. You will learn the litany; there are offerings to be made to the gods of reasonable doubt, presumption of innocence, credibility of witnesses, etc. Develop a way to present the liturgy that works for you and use it in case after case, both to allow you to focus on other things, and to give your stock material a chance to grow and develop in the process.

And, again, focus on keeping it interesting so that you can keep them awake. There's nothing worse than reaching the peak of your argument only to find one or more jurors nodding off. Actually, there is something worse. I had a moon-shine client who suffered from narcolepsy and I turned around in the midst of my wondrous summation only to find him, the actual defendant on trial for his future, fast asleep. At least, I like to think it was the narcolepsy.

And then, of course, there is the final ritual of a trail – waiting for the verdict. I don't know if there is a way to keep this simple. I do know there is no way to keep this pain-free. I found it to be excruciating and it got no better with time and experience. During the wait for the verdict in my first jury trial (guilty), I actually went into the men's room, looked at myself in the mirror, and asked, "Do you really want to do this for the rest of your life?" As time went on, I began to judge the quality of court houses by the lengths of the corridors I could pace as I prayed to the goddess Nicotina.

THIRD COMMANDMENT

QUESTION EVERYTHING [6]

Question everything, especially what you should not have to question. This is important. Your nose should start quivering if the obvious is not obvious. I had it happen with a missing photo.

I took the case of a young woman who had been convicted of beating her 3-year old son to death. The State had charged her and her husband, but it soon became a he said/she said and he said it first, testified against her at the trial and walked away with a minor punishment. The County Medical Examiner testified that the child died of a skull fracture so severe that the M.E., at the autopsy, could insert his pinky finger through the break.

My client was destitute and had been represented by the Public Defender at the trial, but following the conviction,

---

[6] Well, almost everything. You'll probably have the experience of a defendant caught with an ounce of Big Sur sinsemilla that by some alchemical process turns into Mexican Shake when the police introduce it at trial. Let it go!

her family came up with some money for an appeal and hired me. I did the usual – pored over the trial transcript for judicial errors and filed a long brief with the Appellate Court. It was about a one-year wait at that time for oral argument.

In the interim, the case pulled at me. I was really into forensic medicine and was bothered by the disparity between the horrendous nature of the wound described by the M.E., on the one hand, and the fact that the child lived for several days after being admitted to the hospital, on the other. One day, while at the Courthouse on other business, I stopped into see the Prosecutor and he allowed me to search through the autopsy file. I devoured it, grisly photos and all. Except, I could not find a photo of the head wound. Torso photos, extremity photos, long shots, close-ups, but no pictures of this ghastly wound.

That was all I needed. When I think back now, I realize that I must have had cojones the size of cantaloupes. One missing photo and off I went looking for windmills to tilt at. This windmill was the exhumation of a body.

The child had been in the ground almost two years when I started. He was buried in Springfield. Mass., a jurisdiction foreign to me but, fortunately, home to my investigator. Even with his help, it took me over six months. There were applications to be made, motions to be filed, permits to be obtained and the services of an official Medical Examiner in Massachusetts to be secured (and paid for) to preside over the exhumation.

I was also required to hire a funeral director and buy a new casket to rebury the remains. We had long before used up the small retainer she had given us, so I was now essentially spending my law firm's money to do this. My partners were great about it and somehow we pulled this all off without the authorities in NJ knowing about it. I knew they would have contested and turned a difficult process into an impossible one.

The weather was perfect when our little motorcade pulled up to the cemetery – gray, drizzling and clammy. The grave diggers did their work and within an hour, the shattered casket was up on the Medical Examiner's portable table. He examined the skull carefully and it was clean – no fractures – not even a hairline. It was a scene both macabre and ecstatic – I couldn't believe our good fortune.

I returned to New Jersey, filed my papers and, of course, delighted in the firestorm that followed. Since the organs and tissues had decomposed, there was no way to determine the cause of death of the child (it certainly wasn't a skull fracture). The manslaughter charge was dismissed and my client plead guilty to a child neglect charge that brought a minor sentence. It felt right to her because, although she was not the one who abused the child, she did not stop it.

As for the County Medical examiner, there was a grand jury investigation. I was not invited to testify.[7] I don't know what actually happened there, but I heard that the words "male menopause" were used to let him escape with his pension, if not his integrity.

It is in the act of questioning everything that the creative spirit can flourish. "It's always been done this way" is the red flag to your legal bull.

Start with the courtroom:

-- where lawyers sit. In my home county, it was preordained that in a "2-tier" courtroom, where there are two tables, one in front of the other, facing the judge, with the jury on one or the other side, that the defense sat at the front table. This was because, some gazillion years before, a defendant had

---

[7] See the FOURTH COMMANDMENT

physically attacked a prosecutor from the rear. I always thought that being behind me gave my adversaries an advantage. I could not see their faces, body language, or conduct. The prosecutor could have been ogling a juror and I might not know for a while. Before every trial, I made a motion to determine seating position by lottery. I lost every one (motion, not lottery -- there were no lotteries).

-- where the defendant sits. If you want to have some control over the courtroom, don't forget the visual. What do you want the jury to be looking at? Whom do you want the jury to be looking at? In most jurisdictions, there is a tradition, but no fixed rule as to where the defendant sits. If you've got an attractive, or sympathetic one, right there next to you is a good place. If not, what's wrong with the back of the courtroom? (And don't forget to position the family well).

-- there are conventions with language that will not bear scrutiny, no matter how long-established. You are in a forum where words are obviously important. Challenge the ones that don't work for you. For example, you should insist that the prosecutor and request that the judge not dehumanize the defendant by calling him that. Defendants should be referred to by their name. Don't ever let the prosecutor or police use the term "investigation" to describe any activity that took place after your client was arrested. What happens after an arrest is not "investigation" – it is "trial prep." And so forth and so on. Victory, as well as you know who, resides in the details.

Paying attention with an open mind can lead to fresh questions that can make a difference. In a major Mob case, a group of defense lawyers was sitting around listening to tapes of phone calls made by a scum-bag turned government star witness who had confessed to several murders while negotiating himself out of substantial jail time. He was in protective custody, living in a hotel with several State Troopers for a few weeks while awaiting his appearance in our case. As we were listening to hour after unending hour of his banal, egoistic recorded phone calls from custody, my colleague, John, thought he heard the tinkle of ice in a glass and concluded that the guy was drinking a cocktail. We filed a motion for discovery on the issue and the trial judge, a prosecution clone, granted it, figuring that there was no way the government was buying this murderer booze. They were, and the flap that erupted got us a couple of more weeks of pre-trial motions, putting more pressure on the government in our plea-bargain negotiations.

Legislation is always a fertile field for fresh thinking. There are some really stupid laws on the books.

-- Lawyers had been making a good living by defending bookmaking cases for years. The statute in NJ read that it was illegal to "wager on the outcome of a race among horses, mares and geldings." I once argued that the government had failed to prove that the animal named on the betting slip was a "horse, mare or gelding". When the judge retorted that it was obviously a horse, I pointed out that at the racetrack, a "horse" is a word applied to a male, five years and older, and that in the statute, "horse" obviously didn't mean all four-legged equines, otherwise why have the words "mare"(female five years and older) and "gelding"(castrated male)? This animal might have been a "colt "(male younger than five), a "filly" (female younger than five) or even a "ridgling" (male with one testicle) and thus not covered by the statute. Lost. Took it all the way to an Appellate Court. Lost again, but all that effort got me a good plea-bargain eventually.

Sometimes, you can get the system to turn on itself. The main loitering statute in New Jersey in my day was "failure to give a good account." Loitering statutes are important because, aside from their proper use, they are often employed to pursue other goals (politics, manners, revenge, a multitude of law enforcement sins). No one seemed to have ever really questioned this statute and I'm ashamed to say that it took me three cases before I saw the light. In the fourth, I began the cross-examination of the arresting officer by accusing him of failing to give the Miranda warnings. He became immediately defensive and swore that he had. The rest was easy:

"You have charged him with failure to give a good account of himself?"

"Yes I have."

"And are you certain you gave him the Miranda warnings?"

"I absolutely did."

"So you told him he didn't have to say anything."

"Yes I did."

"And then you charged him with the offense of not saying anything?"

It's all about bringing a fresh eye to whatever

situation you are confronted with. Forget about what's been done before. This is you, now, in this unique set of circumstances. You are bringing something new to it. I remember finishing a drunk-driving case in Municipal Court one evening and stopping for a moment to check out my friend Marty who was representing someone for killing too many ducks on a hunting foray. He was arguing that a wounded duck is not a dead duck and pressured the State to produce the fowl bodies, or at least the autopsy reports, so he could engage the issue of cause of death. As I left, I heard him demanding that the State produce the *ducto delecti*.

FOURTH COMMANDMENT

REMEMBER: YOU ARE ALONE

Remember, it's The State v. Jones, not Smith v. Jones. The State, the People – all of them against little ol' you. It's a good thing that "they" are the government or you'd never stand a chance against those odds. After all, it was government in some form or other that made the Susan B. Anthony dollar.

But don't underestimate the power of the government to mess with you if they can get their act together. I had a mega-defendant gangland trial with a long pre-trail motion period. For two months, every day, all of the defendants, their counsel, families, the prosecutors, judge and bailiffs gathered in the courtroom and the scene became very comfortable after a while. In fact, the wives of the defendants brought freshly-cooked Italian food to the courtroom every day and it was shared by the lawyers, prosecutors, and even court personnel. Very comfortable. Until the first day of jury selection, the day all of the prospective jurors were called to court. I arrived at the courthouse to find two police helicopters circling overhead and four Troopers with sniper rifles on the roof of the building. It was a lot to overcome. We didn't.

In this David/Goliath struggle, you are alone. You are on the outside of a community of shared interest. Remember that everyone -- the judge, jury, prosecutor, court stenographer, bailiff, clerk, sergeant-at-arms -- all get their paycheck from the same place -- the government. You don't. That shared interest runs deeper than money. It runs to identification, an identity that you do not share.

What it means:

1. No respect, just like Rodney. Notice the capital letters for Prosecutor, Attorney General, Assistant Attorney General, Deputy Attorney General, District Attorney, Deputy Assistant to the Assistant Deputy of the Acting Prosecutor. You can spend the next millennium in vain looking for defense attorney with initial caps.

Or fake respect. You will find that police officers will call you "Counselor", not as a sign of respect, but to enable them to avoid showing you the respect of addressing you by your last name.

2. No parking spaces. Note any courthouse parking lot. There are parking spaces reserved for the judge,

prosecutor, jury, clerical and custodial personnel, etc. I've never seen them for defense lawyers. I never tilted at this windmill, but there were many occasions where I found myself in resentment when, after trudging across a huge public parking lot with two briefcases and a carton of transcripts, I would nod hello to the Prosecutor as he emerged from his car parked right the frig next to the front door of the Courthouse.

3. Generally, unless you make it happen otherwise, you are on the outside of the gossip hotline. Don't ever underestimate the importance of this. It affects your control of the information flow. How is the judge feeling today? What did Juror #3 say to the bailiff? What was really going on with the rat witness downstairs in the holding pen?

4. Those in power usually got there by being part of the system, not by attacking it as you are often called upon to do. The Prosecutors and Judges are most often cut of the same cloth; either their pants are too short or skirts are too long.

Also, aside from being alone, remember that you have chosen to ply a trade in which you start each endeavor behind the eight ball. A case doesn't start because you think it's a good one. Or because you like your chances. It starts because your adversaries think they have a lock. They have had the opportunity to examine and research the evidence; they have run it by a Grand Jury. They're feeling pretty good. They think they have proof beyond a reasonable doubt!

And, if that's not bad enough, you are embedded in a system that is stacked against you in its day-to-day machinations. Sure, **in general**, the system is weighted toward the defendant because of the burden of proof beyond a reasonable doubt, and, most importantly, the root assumption that it is better that ten innocent persons go free than that one innocent person be convicted. But day-to-day, case-by-case, courthouse-by-courthouse, you will always be climbing uphill because of the attitudes you will meet, the prejudices you will suffer, and the mores you will have to contest.

For example, it's very nice to have a "law" that requires an Indictment to be broken up or "severed" when the case it presents is too complicated for a jury to deal with. It's quite another when a trial judge denies your Motion to Sever in a case which has nine defendants, eight of whom have the same last name, four of whom have the same first name, charged with five murders, three conspiracies and over one hundred armed robberies. Somehow, the judge did not think it would be problem for the jury, who were not allowed to take notes, to remember after eight months of trial that it was PR Jones, not PC Jones, in the bar on 12th Street, on June 12, 1972 for Armed Robbery #82, while PS and PA Jones were the ones supposed to be at Armed Robbery #106 on October 12th. He looked at me with a straight face when he made this decision not to break up the Indictment. This was the same judge who could not tell the defendants apart after four months of daily pre-trial motions. And he could take notes!

It's really great to not be alone, though, when there is a true and necessary community of vested interests in a multi-defendant case. You become like a theater troupe, a football team, or a military unit – showing up each day for the length of the tour, season, or campaign, to make your unique contribution to the scene, game, or battle. The friendship, community, trust, humor, intimacy, diversity and bonds that accompany a well-coordinated defense can often make all of the "aloneness" worthwhile. To paraphrase the great jurist Lily Tomlin, it's great to have someone to be alone with together.

But, no matter how closely-connected the defense

may be, your primary duty, of course, is to your client. Keep your eye on the bottom line -- Can I get out if everyone else goes down?

FIFTH COMMANDMENT

KEEP TIME

As with most human endeavors, time is a crucial factor in so much of what you will be doing. If not a factor, certainly an issue that should always be addressed directly and consciously. At the very least, look at the basic question: Is time on my side?

-- Will the government's case get better or worse with time? In other words, do you want to delay or push the start of the trial. Is the government's main witness old? Infirm? In a mega-defendant gangland trial I had, the defense kept the prosecutor at bay from September to January with motions, hearings and jury selection. If I ever write a book about that case, I'm going to call it *Four Months of Foreplay*. It's awfully hard for anyone, even the government, to keep a case together for four months.

-- Should the trial itself be long or short? This can change, of course, as things develop, but a trial has a tone, a rhythm and you want to make sure that it serves you. Sometimes, a slow, delay-filled rhythm is all you can muster to try to stop the government's momentum.

-- Should the stay of the defendant or any witness on the stand be protracted or brief? In other words, will he or she wear well with the jury?

There is the timing of motions, of objections, introduction of exhibits - -all should be conscious decisions. There is the time it takes to retrieve a note from your file, computer or briefcase while 24 eyes are glued to your fumbling. There is the timing of a trial day, of morning breaks and luncheon recesses that could impact something you are doing or trying to stop, or that could leave the jury in a place that you do or do not want them to be left. There is the timing of the trial calendar. In the mercy-killing case, we ended the testimony on Friday (not good time-management on my part). I moved to convene the trial on Saturday to avoid my jurors hearing those Sunday sermons on the quality of life. Motion denied.

Sometimes, or maybe often, time is all you've got. I once defended someone for the actual crime of wearing a mini-skirt. It was a guy and the Asbury Park, NJ ordinance he offended declared that it was an offense "to appear in public in the clothing of the opposite gender." I had gotten a call from a newspaper reporter who had just seen a Municipal Court judge sentence an eighteen-year old kid to ninety days in the County jail for this offense. Can you imagine what happens to a kid like this in the County jail for ninety days? Can you imagine what was going through the judge's mind? Of course, this was rural New Jersey in the mid '60's. He either thought the defendant deserved this punishment or that it would cure him of his disease.

I took the case, got my client out on bail and filed an Appeal, which would get us a brand-new trial in County Court, fresh testimony and all. My only hope, of course, was to have the Ordinance declared unconstitutional. He was wearing a mini-skirt, cape, mesh stockings and ballet slippers.

On the day of the trial, I knew there was one thing up my sleeve, but that it would evaporate if the trial were adjourned. So, of course, the first thing I did was make a motion for adjournment (I had learned early on that, as a criminal defense lawyer, if there is something you don't want to happen, it's probably a good idea to ask for it). This, of course, outraged the Prosecutor. Although my initial presentation was purposively weak, it grew in subsequent offerings as the Prosecutor became more insistent and as I could sense the judge moving to his side.

The intensity of the debate ended when the judge turned to me in a loud voice and declared: "THIS CASE WILL BE TRIED TODAY!"

I then began my argument on the constitutionality of the Ordinance–

– it was too broad, covering such innocent conduct as the judge's wife going to a Halloween party dressed as Attila the Hun (I probably could have used a better example); the ordinance could have been tailored, for example, to relate to people who cross-dress to escape apprehension;

– it was unclear as to what conduct it prohibited. What is "clothing of the opposite gender?" In those days, my wife wore khaki pants, white oxford shirt and loafers. What gave gender to pants? The location of the zipper?

I realized that I wasn't getting anywhere when the judge cited some portion of the Bible that said "a man shall not dress in the clothing of a woman because it is an abomination in the eyes of the Lord." (The Abomination course was not offered at my law school.) On that note, he declared a recess and invited us into chambers.

In chambers, the judge asked the Prosecutor about

the length of the trial. He responded that this would be the shortest criminal presentation in history. One sentence of testimony by the police officer. "I saw him walking down the street in a mini-skirt."

The judge asked for my response.

"I'll object," I said.

"On what basis," the judge asked. "This is personal and relevant eye-witness observation."

"I'll object to the word 'him'. It's the government's obligation to prove every element of its case beyond a reasonable doubt. Before they can prove my client was wearing clothing of the opposite gender, they first must prove what gender my client is."

"Easy." said the judge. "I'll just bring the defendant into chambers for an examination."

"Not good enough for proof beyond a reasonable doubt," I countered. "Genitalia do not prove gender. That's not what they look at in the Olympics. You've got to look at a cell and check the chromosomes – it's either XX or XY. Very simple. Take a scraping from somewhere easy (mucous membrane inside the cheek), put it under the microscope............"

"We can do that," the Prosecutor said. "We'll just get an adjournm........"

He couldn't even get the word out of his mouth when I reminded him that THIS CASE WAS GOING TO BE TRIED TODAY!

The judge threw us out of chambers, went back on the bench and ruled the Ordinance unconstitutional. Once "time" became the determinant in the case, once time became the turf, the defense had it made.

SIXTH COMMANDMENT

PLAY THE GAME ON YOUR TURF

This is the same as not picking a fight you can't win.

Stay on your turf with the theme of the case. The idea is to find an issue that you are strong on (not an easy task in many cases) and make that the most important issue in the case. It may not be the most relevant issue or the most glamorous issue – just make it seem like the most important. You do that with your time and attention and energy and attitude. When the jury leaves the box for deliberations, they should believe that the way they decide that issue is the way they should decide the case.

I used to see the reverse of this in many bookmaking cases. I'd watch a defense lawyer (in a case where the offense was the possession of gambling paraphernalia) spend ego-filled hours grilling the government's expert witness on whether the slip of paper containing date, amount, name of horse, odds, etc. was or was not in fact a "betting slip". All *good time* for the prosecution. By the time the case was over, the jury went to deliberations believing that the only issue to be decided was whether this was a betting slip. A losing issue. Better to focus on whether the possession was "knowing" or why the government didn't call a handwriting expert or anything else you can dream of. The government always enters the game with a whole store of *good time* in its pocket. Don't just give them more. Make them earn it.

Is your turf factual? Emotional? Procedural? If you have the facts on your side (a rare occasion), keep the trial to the facts – quickly, clearly, directly. If all you have is emotion, then slop up the joint.

Stay on your turf when examining a witness. Each witness -- you know where you are strong and where you are weak. Stay with your strength. You are in control. And this especially holds true for an expert. Grant that they know more about the subject matter than you do. In my experience, arrogance precedes a fall more often than pride. I had an expert eat my lunch once when, during my cross-examination, he subtly shifted the basis of the testimony from an area of ballistics I had studied to one I had not. I was young and full of hormones then. I got over it.

Sometimes, you're just stuck and you can't find your turf in the substance of the case or in the procedure. You might still get lucky if you continue to focus on where you might have the advantage. I once represented a quadriplegic who was arrested in his bed at home for possession of marijuana. I know that sounds unbelievable, but it happened. All-plegics, quadri-or para-, need to take muscle relaxants; otherwise their muscles can go into violent and spontaneous spasm with sufficient force to snap a limb or throw them out of bed. The drug of choice in these situations is Valium, a horribly debilitating medication that even the manufacturer suggests not be taken for more than a few months at a time. Valium didn't work for my client; it constipated him (the last thing someone in this condition needed) and put him into what he called "the ozone layer", unable to function or relate even in his limited state.

He used marijuana because it did not constipate him, it gave him an appetite (a/k/a the "munchies"), and allowed him to function – in fact, with the use of marijuana, he completed a computer course by punching the keyboard with a pencil between his teeth.

My defense was necessity, medical necessity.

Necessity is always a defense to a criminal charge. You can drive on the shoulder of the highway if you need to steer clear of an accident in front of you. You can bring a boat laden with dangerous cargo into a port that forbids dangerous cargo if you are caught in a hurricane. My point was that my guy had no viable choice but to smoke dope.

I lost the case after taking it all the way to the NJ Supreme Court. It's much too complicated to explain here, but, I think, when all is said and done, that what did me in was the deeply-ingrained, long-standing, Blackwellian jurisprudential principle "Ain't nobody smokin' no legal dope in New Jersey, no way, no how." So, when all is said and done, in New Jersey, you can kill someone if you have to (self-defense). But, you can't smoke dope if you have to. Go figure!

But it wasn't over yet. When the case was called for trial, I showed up alone. The judge asked about the presence of the defendant and I said that he wanted to be in Court, but could not manage it. He was, after all, quadriplegic. The judge said he would send a Sheriff's car for him. "Not good enough," I argued. "You will need an ambulance and several attendants to do it properly and safely." I could see his budgetary wheels spinning.

"Beyond that," I argued, "when he does arrive, I will place on the record that he is being deprived of his right to be present at his trial. His body will be here, but he won't. He cannot leave the house without a muscle relaxant and, if he could take marijuana, he would be 'present'. But since the State is requiring him to take Valium, he will be spending his time in the ozone layer, not in Court."

The case was placed on the inactive list.

SEVENTH COMMANDMENT

NEVER START DOWN A ROAD YOU WON'T
GET TO THE END OF [8]

I learned this one pretty directly. I got a porn case --
magazines, a few nudist periodicals, but mostly male-oriented
still photos, most with "partials" (the slim line between art and
pornography to my client was determined by whether the erection
was partial or total). The stuff wasn't really that bad, especially by
today's standards. A little sunbathing, a little shower activity. No
actual sex. But, it was the '60's, and it was suburban/rural New
Jersey, and, other than attacking the search warrant, I couldn't
figure out a way to defend the case other than to try to use the
trial to convince the jury that the material was not "obscene."

I began to develop my approach to the trial when
a law clerk told me he had just seen a Swedish film at the local
Art House and that, in his opinion, the film was much more
"obscene" than the stuff we were defending in the porn case. I
had to check it out, of course, and felt the same way. Eureka! I'll

---

[8] This COMMANDMENT may be violated out of desperation
(probably often)

just change the psychological set of the jury -- inundate them with really bad porno and my client's stuff will pale by comparison. I gave the clerk the assignment of procuring the worst pornography he could find and did he ever – including some memorable dog and pig pictorial adventures. I figured that at the trial, I could begin to introduce this material during my cross of the State's obscenity expert and eventually lower the bar of decency with my glut of materials.

Of course, somehow the case was assigned to Judge Jones, a/k/a "The Great Catholic", a stern man of unquenchable righteousness. I first ran into him in a sensational case of some government employees, i.e., firemen, who were charged with having group sex with a woman while on duty in the firehouse (an offense I like to call "Misconduct in Orifice"). The defense lawyers were going over the written statements of the victim and I asked, "Who's going to explain to the jury what a BJ is?" A colleague answered, "Who's going to explain it to Judge Jones?"

Well, during the porn trial, the cross of the expert, a rigid psychologist of strong moral fiber, went well. Since there was no actual sex depicted in my client's material, it could only be the nudity that was obscene and soon the psychologist had backed himself in a corner called "nudity = obscenity". Which brought me to Michelangelo's Statue of David which brought the judge roaring out of the box for a little rehabilitation. Anyway, I started to introduce my little nest egg – not the worst, but pretty offensive. The judge cut me off pretty quickly as he saw the jury's offended and disgusted reaction and ruled that no more material of that nature would be introduced. I certainly don't know, in retrospect, whether I would have been any more successful if I had gotten to go all the way, but the only psychological set of the jury I was able to change was the one that brings on anger. It was the quickest verdict of guilt I ever had – the jury was out for thirty-one minutes.

For his offense, Judge Jones sentenced my client to not less than to 14 and not more than 21 years in the State Penitentiary (that very morning, a manslaughter client was sentenced to 6 months). I think he was offended. Fortunately, it was all reversed on appeal on the search warrant.

The point of disciplined compliance with this Commandment is that it gives you a useful perspective to focus on each task. Where do I want to end up? How will I get there?

Each task. The rule lives not only in the broad strokes of strategy, but also in the details, the tasks. It's in your Opening Statement, where you do not make promises you cannot keep and where you leave your skeletons in the closet only if you are absolutely sure that they will not jump out and bite you later in the trial. It's in your approach to each witness, requiring you to narrow each inquiry to exactly what you want from what you know is available. From what you <u>know</u> is available. There's no flailing in trying criminal cases. Know where you are going and how you are going to get there.

The longer I tried cases, the more foreign it became to me to question a witness on the fly, spontaneously, looking to see what I might find. It simply rarely pays to go foraging off into the unknown, down an unknown road to an unknown destination. I was cured of any tendency to the contrary during the cross-examination of a pathologist in a murder case, who had just completed reciting his impressive qualifications for the Assistant Medical Examiner position he occupied. He was filling in for Dr. Big, the Medical Examiner himself, who was a legend in the field. As I was leaving my seat, my investigator leaned over and said, "That's bullshit. He got the position because he's Dr. Big's son-in-law."

I went after it, some snide questions about his "glorious" qualifications, leading to the and-isn't-it-true-that-you're-Dr.Big's-son-in-law, to which he replied "No." Clunk! I was stunned (even more so when I turned and saw my investigator slowly pushing his chair from the defense table as if he were getting up to leave); this isn't something the guy could be lying about. Of course, I never should have gone for the spontaneous, but it was such a tasty opportunity. Fortunately, I had the good sense to apologize – basically, I stopped the trial, turned to the witness and apologized, and I think the jury and judge appreciated that.

In my day, when I prepared to cross examine experts, I wanted to see every book they had written, every article published, every speech made. I had to go to the library and deal with things like the Dewey Decimal System. You are so fortunate these days. A little Google and Jeeves and you could find out what these people eat for dinner, not to mention the names, addresses, and maybe social security numbers of their fathers-in-law.

I had to take a chance once – on Direct

Examination, you know, the one thing that is supposed to be totally scripted. I had to. I was desperate. In a murder trial, my defendant was testifying for his life, but during the entire Direct Examination, he rested his elbow on the ledge of the witness stand and rested his head on his hand. I could see the jury totally turned off by his apparent nonchalance and dared, as my final question, to ask him why he was so positioned. "I'm so nervous," he said, "that I have to hold my head to keep it from trembling." Thank you, lord!

EIGHTH COMMANDMENT

MAKE YOUR WEAKNESS YOUR STRENGTH

Of course, as a general reality, you are usually the weaker of the two sides in the courtroom when it comes to resources and assets. You play that card as often as you can. "The government, with all of its resources, could only come up with...." "If only the defense had the ability to muster squads of detectives,...." Really – you are the underdog. Work it!

Your weaknesses, if they can't be hidden, must, at least, be explained and, at best, exploited. At its most obvious, I once had the opportunity to use my client's homosexuality as a defense in a rape case (Yes, homosexuality was a major "weakness" in that trial. To that jury, "gay" equaled "leper."). No great stroke of genius that, but the mechanism is the same no matter the context. If you have a less than intelligent client that you must put on the stand, you can make his dimness a shield against an aggressive cross by the prosecutor. You can set it up with the jury that way on Opening. There's nothing more satisfying than the alchemy of turning dross into gold.

I learned this the most deeply in a murder case

involving an Army Staff Sergeant charged with murdering his wife by shooting her. From a defense standpoint, the facts were horrific. He and his wife were in the bedroom with the door closed. His mother-in-law was in the living room, heard a loud argument, a shot and, when she ran into the bedroom, saw the sergeant, kneeling on the floor with the gun in his hand, and cradling the inert body of his wife across his lap. When questioned after the arrest, the defendant said that he was standing by the dresser, arguing with his wife, when she pulled the gun out from under the mattress and shot herself in the side. He responded to the officer's prodding by explaining that he saw her shoot herself in the right side with the gun in her right hand. Unfortunately for us, the fatal bullet wound was on the left. So, not only was my client supposed to be a murderer, he was a liar as well and not a very good one at that.

At first there appeared to be a crack in the government's case around the issue of cause of death. The wife died in the hospital three days after the shooting. The operation to remove the bullet was done on the first day. Interestingly enough, the X-rays at the time of the operation showed another bullet lodged in her body. Seems that she had been shot by her first husband some years before, a fact I had trouble dealing with since I couldn't figure out if it was good or bad for us.

Following surgery, she was instructed by the doctors to move – to walk, use her extremities; otherwise, she stood a good chance of developing a blood clot that could cause her harm. Well, she refused to move for three days, claiming paralysis although the nurses would occasionally see her move when she thought they were not looking. It was an act of defiant will. She was not going to move. She didn't and died from a blood clot that traveled to her lung. You can see how desperate I was. She didn't die from the gunshot wound; she died committing suicide by refusing to move. Yech! I regained my senses.

I did end up fouling up the courtroom a little with the prior shooting. I felt that any negative energy I could cast around her would help my guy a little. The real reason for doing it though was that it gave me a chance to use the sergeant's father as a witness. His name was Bunion and he had never before been out of Alabama. And, yes he did wear overalls. And yes, he did roll his own out of a Prince Albert can. And, yes, his serenity, intelligence and dignity did wonders for the atmosphere around our defense.

Which, by the way, was to make the sergeant's "wrong" description of the event the foundation of the defense. I made a lot of my client's so-called "right hand/left hand" lie during the cross-examination of the investigating police officers. I also used them to bring the bedroom to life, to describe the location of the bed, the chair, the dresser, the mirror over the dresser, the painting of Christ next to that, etc.

The defense testimony was by Bunion, on the righteousness of his son and the opposite of his daughter-in-law, and the sergeant himself, who repeated that he was standing by the dresser when she shot herself in the right side with her right hand. Although I never said a word about it directly during any of the testimony, the jury began to get the picture (as I'm sure you have by now) and I was able to stand up on Summation and collect payment on a notion that they had come to themselves: "No one would tell such a lie. The very fact that he would say 'right' instead of 'left' is proof that he was not looking directly at his wife when she drew the gun from under the mattress (probably to put it behind her back). He was looking through the mirror and that is the image that is engraved in his memory. The so-called 'lie' is the very proof that he was at the dresser and not on the bed."

I was delighted for the sergeant when the jury came back with an acquittal. He had convinced me of his innocence when, before trial, he turned down an amazing plea-bargain offer of some minor manslaughter conviction and no jail time. NO JAIL TIME. He told me that he didn't shoot her and couldn't say that he did, even if it meant a free walk.

Just keeping this perspective in mind can help. Focus on your weakest point. Is there anything you can do about it? I got close another time in a municipal corruption scandal. My building contractor client was charged with bribing a city official to ease the way on some real estate development. The official had been "turned" earlier and was wired for his meeting with my client. The tape was just plain awful. Basically, the official asks for the bribe and my client says yes. I was looking into an entrapment defense(the place you go when there is no other place to go), but my guy had jumped so quickly on the tape, it would be hard to sell that he was imposed upon.

My client had a concentration-camp tattoo on his arm and explained that was where he spent his childhood. I realized that this man's psyche had been formed in an astoundingly authoritative, not to mention horrific, atmosphere. The entrapment defense would allow the argument that he would respond to authority differently from someone raised in this country. The person in authority said "Pay me" and he would be primed to jump. Interesting, but I never got to use the immediacy of his response as our strength as opposed to our downfall. The prosecutor didn't want to deal with it and gave us a good plea.

It's just like the 14-point play in football when the other team is about to score from your 1-yard line and you pick up a fumble and run 99 yards for a score. Look what Streisand and Durante did with their noses. Or Woody Allen with his nerdy neuroses.

You might even be able to turn to your advantage the fact that you are alone in the system. The good part of being alone is that you don't have to fit in, or pretend to fit in, or try to fit in. You might make the role of outsider work for you, not only in the independence and freedom that it brings, but also in the details. Like the courthouse gossip. There are a lot of disgruntled and bored courthouse employees and officials who will bond with you in a moment for the sake of a little taste of the spirit of rebellion against the system that made them disgruntled and bored in the first place.

NINTH COMMANDMENT

BE PREPARED

I hate to break it to you, but the Boy Scouts were right. Be prepared! It's the way. It's the only way. Other than *bad time*, surprise is your most deadly enemy. In this age of pre-trial discovery, if you are surprised in the courtroom, you are guilty of malpractice. Don't even bother to look for another explanation.

I always had confidence that I was bright and well-educated. So, I figured that if I could work harder than my adversary, I'd have it made. I lost my innocence in this respect, though, when I got the case of the guy charged with attempted arson. The State alleged that my client, of all people, was responsible for the situation they found in an Asbury Park hotel (it was February, of course); the hallways were lined with garbage cans filled with gasoline, as were the stopped-up sinks and toilets. All of my native intelligence, exquisite training and diligent, if not obsessive, hard work, were simply overwhelmed by the incontrovertible fact that my client had charged the 600 gallons of gasoline to his personal credit card. My challenge ("It can't be him. No-one can be that stupid.") was met by the jury with a resounding, "Yes he can!"

But other than the total "shit-ems"[9], preparation is the key. I've seen very few cases that were "won" in the courtroom. I won most of mine in the shower, library, or, unfortunately, driving on my way to court. In fact, I used to be totally opposed to the concept of Bar Exams because they test lawyers to do what lawyers should never do – think on their feet (except, of course, evidentiary questions that arise during a trial). But, then I became an Assistant Bar Examiner during a time when the exam was all essay questions and the first blue book I opened to grade began an answer with: "This is against the law of God as handed down through Moses." Maybe Bar Exams aren't such a bad idea after all.

Being prepared isn't always easy. I represented a very petite woman married to a 6', 7", 275 pound defensive lineman for an NFL team. One night, after what she claimed were years of physical abuse, she slit his throat while he was sleeping.

---

[9] A '60's term for cases you couldn't win if you tried them a hundred times.

He awoke and died while on the phone with 911. I had to listen over and over to the tape of that call, I had to actually listen to him die again and again, just to make sure that I was prepared for anything on it that the State might use against us or that I might find in our favor. She fired me shortly before the trial, but not soon enough to save me from that ordeal.

Being anally-retentive and obsessive/compulsive, I loved the preparation part of the process; poring over transcripts, police reports, autopsy reports, lab reports, phone records, diaries; the battle against surprise, the methodical work, the planning, research, and flights of creative fancy. It was all like collecting and storing ammunition, savoring each favorable fact or argument, getting myself armed and dangerous. And visualizing. I visualized a lot, imagining a witness on the stand and how it might progress. I tried always to think of everything and often did, except for the numbers runner with a catheter. I knew he had a catheter, of course, but just did not anticipate how the pressure of being in a courtroom would affect the frequency of the bag-emptying procedure, which interrupted every run of momentum I was trying to build in the case.

Once you are in the courtroom, i urge you to take

notes of the things you did not anticipate. I started a personal "trial emergency book" shortly into my career. Every time something came up in the courtroom (some legal or evidentiary point) that I was not prepared for, I went back to the office, researched it and put the references in this loose-leaf notebook. Every once in a while, maybe two years after an entry, the situation would arise again in the courtroom and I'd be right there with a citation. Yeah! Not as good as sex, but an exciting and fulfilling experience, nevertheless. This book got to be very valuable after a while, and very thick. Sort of a record of or testament to my unpreparedness. Now I'm kicking myself for not selling this when I retired. I probably could have retired earlier.

My obsession with preparation reached its peak in a case I had of a couple of "mules"[10] who were caught in South Jersey with sixty-six pounds of grass (a lot, in those days, for which they faced an incredibly stiff jail sentence), wrapped in three, separate, twenty-two-pound packages. It was an ingenious

---

[10] "Mules", in the '70's, were people who drove marijuana up the Eastern seaboard, from Florida to New York City. They were often college kids making a few extra bucks when they were going home anyway.

system. First the twenty-two-pound, compressed clump was put in a 3-mil *Hefty* bag, the bag was sealed and placed in another *Hefty* bag. *Lysol* and some other such stuff was sprayed heavily, and then the second bag was sealed. This was now placed in a 3rd *Hefty* bag, sprayed and sealed. At the end, the package was placed in a carton and sealed with duct tape.

My mules (a couple of 20-year-olds from Miami U) had just come over the Delaware Memorial Bridge and were stopped by a State Trooper immediately on the Jersey side. They were ordered out of the car and the Trooper searched and found the three cartons under all of their luggage, books, bedding, etc.

The outcome of the case, of course, depended on the legality of the search. Our only hope was to get the evidence suppressed. We knew that this was what is called today a "profiling" situation. The NJ State Troopers were automatically stopping and searching cars with Florida plates driven by long-hairs. Since, in fact, the Trooper had no cause to stop and search the vehicle as he did, he would have to come up with some story it would be my job to attack. By the way, these "stories" (reasons to search a vehicle) rode waves of fashion that rivaled skirt lengths. For a while, every time a Trooper stopped a car, he was able to see brownish-green, vegetative matter protruding from under the front seat as he looked through the driver's window without entering the car. Then came the "dropsy" fad. The officers would observe something dropped or thrown from the car window as they approached. Then for a few years it seemed that every drug dealer in New Jersey decided to give his consent to a vehicle search.

The one the Trooper picked in this case was a beauty. The Police Report indicated that he had stopped the vehicle for a routine motor vehicle check and as he approached the driver's window to get a license, he smelled the overpowering odor of non-burning marijuana, which, of course, gave him probable cause to order the occupants out and search the vehicle.

My first thought was to contact the **3-M** company. They must have done some research on the odor-retention qualities of their 3-mil *Hefty* bags. I struck out. They had done a lot of work on tensile strength, but not a whit on what I needed.

So I went to Plan B. On the day of the Motion to Suppress, I arrived at court with a carton that contained 10 pounds of dead fish, wrapped in three, 3-mil *Hefty* bags, sprayed, carton, duct tape, etc. I placed the carton under the front of the judge's bench and proceeded with the hearing. The officer testified as expected, and I cross-examined him intensely on the conditions that his nose was operating under. He was not in a four-wall enclosed room like the one we were in. He was out in the open air, wind blowing, trucks going by at 60 mph, etc., etc., etc.

After a few of hours of testimony and argument, the judge was ready to rule. I stopped him to point out the carton under his bench. He said he had noticed it and asked what that had to do with the case. With a flourish (I couldn't resist), I signaled my clerk who entered the courtroom wheeling a large garbage can. I then slit open the carton and bags, and the smell that instantly permeated the entire courtroom was simply and wonderfully and egregiously and offensively and righteously and totally noxious.

After making use of the garbage can, I told the judge that this package had been under his nose for several hours in a tightly sealed courtroom and he didn't catch even a drift of the dead fish. Immediately upon recovering his dignity, he granted the Motion to Suppress, the case was over and the kids went on to finish college.

I tell this story because it's fun and, I guess, because it turned out so well. But the point is preparation. What a metaphor. These fish were wrapped in everything I ever believed about preparation. It's hard to describe the hours we had to put in to get the timing right. We had a first-year law student, Dennis, clerking with us for the summer, who never knew what hit him when he spent a couple of weeks of his "legal" training calibrating the aroma of dead fish. We worked for those two weeks, buying fresh dead fish in the morning, packaging them in the *Hefty* bags, storing them in the office law library under temperature conditions that we hoped would meet those of the courtroom. We started at five hours and I forget the outer limit, but there did come a point in time when those fish smelled quite intensely through the *Hefty* bags, not to mention my partners' offices.

The idea, of course, was that the package had to not smell at all when closed and immediately and intensely reek when opened. We got it down to where we felt comfortable with a window of 2 hours. I had to draw out my cross-examination of the Trooper and ask for a couple of recesses to give the fish time to fester. But we got it right thanks to Dennis's hard work. We bought him a fishing rod as a going-away present when he went back to law school in the fall.

What's gonna come, what could possibly come, what should never come. Preparing for trial is like writing a screenplay, although the actors don't always behave and read the right lines. You can't plan the Prosecutor's script, but you can be ready to deal with it.

Being prepared means researching the law, studying the facts, etc. But it also means being prepared physically. Like any endeavor, trying criminal cases involves health, stamina and sobriety.

Watch out for the lunchtime drink. It's so seductive. There's so much tension and pressure and that "one" drink at lunch can do wonders for the spirit. I saw it happen to a lot of my colleagues. In fact, the lawyer's table at the local lunch spot had its internal clock for the end of the lunch recess. We knew it was time to go back to court when Bill Jones' face fell into the soup bowl. You don't want to be Bill Jones.

This was my inner police officer. If I'm ordering a

drink at lunch, I'm in trouble. I violated this rule once. It was my first case against this particular Deputy Attorney General and when the jury was sent out to deliberate late in the afternoon, she and I decided to have dinner and a drink with my co-counsel. It was a complicated case and the jury would be out for hours, if not days. And it was late afternoon. It wasn't actually lunch. Just one martini, but I'm a cheap date and was feeling it when the bailiff came into the restaurant to tell us that the jury had "knocked " with a question. Wouldn't you know it! I survived, but I never violated the rule again.

TENTH COMMANDMENT

RESPECT THE PROCESS

Respect the process. Honor the process. It is a process, the process of advocacy, of selling a position. You're not just trying cases; you are practicing the art of advocacy. It has an order, it has rules, it has boundaries that should be seen before pushed. There is a "right" way to do things. Not "right" in the sense of moral, but in the sense of efficient, effective – a way that increases the odds of you getting what you want.

This applies to legal arguments as well as factual presentations. It doesn't matter whether you are arguing to judges or juries; your first goal, other than keeping them awake, is to get them to want to decide in your favor and your second is to show them how.

Don't forget about that first one. Getting someone to want you to win is delicate, especially in an arena that frowns upon the emotional aspects of life. How can you do that? By focusing on it, by being conscious of it as a goal, by addressing it directly when you contemplate your presentation of a case, a witness, an argument. It may be the things you present. It may be the things you don't. Just remember, whether you are dressing up an argument in a brief or dressing up a defendant for a courtroom appearance, you are trying to win someone over and it's much easier to push them in a certain direction if they are already moving that way.

The process is the process, but the beautiful thing about your craft is that you get to practice it in a constantly changing myriad of contexts, bodies of substantive knowledge that you are required to grasp, retain and use. It might be forensic medicine (I used to spend hours in the basement of the NYC Medical Examiner's Office watching autopsies,[11] trying to learn why a pathologist could pick out a sub-dural hematoma from a photo full of blood and tissue that looked like reddish-brown finger painting to me). It might be the science of fingerprinting, or chemistry, or ballistics, or blood-typing or arson investigation. It might be cost-accounting in a white-collar crime or the role of the vig in a bookmaking case. It can all be fascinating if you allow it to be. Rich areas of facts, theories, figures, lore that you get to immerse yourself in and then figure out how to use.

---

[11] I never understood my stomach for this; when it comes to a live person, I am squeamish about a cut on the finger.

Part of respecting the process is respecting your clients, some of whom are just like you, only a little less fortunate. There's no need to judge them. They pay the folks in the black robes for that. Respect your clients, but don't identify with them. Your job is to represent them in a finite endeavor, not be their friend, confidante, etc. I've seen it happen to several criminal defense lawyers. They start dressing like their clients, start talking like their clients. It happens mostly in drug and Mob cases. I knew a guy who tried only two bookmaking cases before he started buying silk suits. The road into this trap is paved with lucre. A client wants to give you a color tv set, get you a hooker, send you some of those wonderful T-bones that just fell off a truck, buy you a drink. There were times when I realized my client wasn't really as interested in buying me a drink as he was in being seen buying me a drink. This gave him prestige in his community. Be careful! What starts as access can quickly become leverage, if not control.

And don't identify with the crime either. You are not the criminal and you are not the crime that has been charged. Although I never really struggled in this respect, I know that this is not always easy. I felt it deeply one time when I was speaking at a law school in Florida and a young, female student asked me how I could represent a man who beat his wife. She could never do that. Part of me understood her conflict and I suggested that she might focus her career in a single-cause way, like house-counsel to an Institute that served her feelings.

The major part of me demurred. I always felt that once I hung out my shingle, I was a cog in the wheel, plying my part in the process without regard to the unseemly contexts that might be involved. I had a role to play; I defended. My client was not a wife-beater until a jury said he was a wife-beater. And what the jury said would not be reliable unless both sides were well-represented and heard. All I had to do was make sure that my client was well-represented and heard. Great strokes of jurisprudential doctrine have often been forged at the impetus of sordid little defendants in ugly cases. I never met Willie Miranda, but I have the feeling he's not Mother Theresa. And, after all, what kind of system would it be if an African-American accused of raping the white Mayor's daughter in a small town in Mississippi in the '60's had to find someone to believe in him in order to have a defense?

This does not mean that it always feels good. Child

molesters were the hardest for me. But I am not a child molester and I do not advocate or suffer kindly child molestation. Nor do I promote wife-beating if I represent someone accused of that. Nor am I a proponent of careless driving, rape, murder, driving while under the influence, the Mob, assault, loitering, littering, burglary, arson, forgery, child neglect, criminal conspiracy, armed robbery, breaking and entering, theft, usury, child abuse, mail fraud, wire fraud, contempt of court, misconduct in office, extortion, bribery or trespass, to name a few of the cases I've defended.

I know, though, that I found a way to cheat in my romantic I'm-a-gun-for-hire philosophy. Looking back, I can see that if a case tugged at my heart and mind, there was always a way to reduce my fee for those who could not afford the rate. I never did that for the you-know-who's. And if I took a case for nothing, I totally felt that I had the right to pick and choose. It all now feels like some form of reverse prostitution. I never compromised my principles for money. I compromised my money for principles. Maybe it's not so reverse.

On the other hand, one of the most wonderful happenstances of this line of work is that you do get to meet and work with a diverse range of people who are basically decent but have compromised themselves by need or greed, or who have been compromised by injustice. Talk about a demographic melting pot. My cases brought me into the families, homes, cultures and communities of Greeks, Italians, Irish, Africans, Armenians, African-Americans, Jamaicans, Poles, Haitians, Albanians, Russians, Buddhists, Catholics, Hindus, Jews, Rosicrucians, Rastafarians, Muslims, Druids, Protestants, Santerians, Pagans, Republicans, Democrats, Independents, Greens, Libertarians, Communists, Socialists (I never had a Fascist), heterosexuals, homosexuals, bisexuals, transsexuals, – to name another few.[12]

Respect the judges. This can be difficult. A lot of them don't deserve it. They come to think they were anointed, not appointed. You know they've turned a corner when they start referring to themselves in the third person. But, it's like any other

---

[12] Ethnicity can be important to your "bedside manner" because it defines your client's experiences and expectations. During the Asbury Park riots in the '60's, I received a call from a Haitian woman whose husband was arrested in a sweep. Over the next three hours, while I tried to arrange bail, I received 14 more calls from her. It took me a while to realize that the source of her panic was that in Haiti in those days (and maybe now), the arrest of a person might mean that you never saw them again.

trade, actually. How many really good plumbers do you know? Anyway, it's the position you show respect, not the person.

I don't know what your expectations are here. You spend all of your time in law school reading Marshall and Brandeis and it might seem after a while that people like that are sitting in the County Criminal Court. Not! You'll never experience this, but I tried cases in front of a non-lawyer judge who owned the hardware store over which Municipal court was located.

Dealing with judges in the courtroom is easy. The rules are fixed and predictable. They are in charge. You submit. How to relate to judges in chambers is a lot more difficult. What will you do when a judge is boring the crap out of you in chambers with some long-winded, unfunny joke and all you want is for her to approve the sensational plea-bargain you just reached with the prosecutor? You laugh at the joke.

It could be worse. In my very first year of practice, I was sitting in the lawyer's lounge, waiting for a plea-bargain conference with a judge in a stabbing case that arose in a community famous for them, when I asked another lawyer what amount of jail time I should settle for. He turned to me and said: "Don't worry about this one. Judge Jones will look it over and say

– 'It's just a couple of niggers stabbing each other. I'll fine him $50 and send him home." Before I could recover my equilibrium, I was in chambers and that was exactly what Judge Jones said after the prosecutor and I explained the case to him. Wow! What a totally radical choice for a rookie. I could get all upset and righteous and my client would do 364 days in the county jail. Or I could swallow my disgust and my client goes home. I swallowed and it sticks in my throat – to this day. My only saving grace was that he was set to retire in 2 months, although, at that time, I probably would have made the same decision even if he were 30 years old.

Your client's well-being is the Catch-22 in your dealings with judges, in and out of the courtroom. In side-bars, at cocktail parties, during bar Association meetings and so on, it is always the fear that your short- or long-term relationship with a judge could hurt your present or future clients, even down to the ugly details. All of the defense lawyers in my county knew that you did not exercise a peremptory challenge on a young, female, short-skirted jury prospect who was seated in the front row of the box when the case was being handled by another Judge Jones, this one semi-lecherous. I have, on occasion, given up my self-respect, dignity and Knicks tickets if I thought it would help my client's cause.

It's also important to respect your adversaries. They are your opponents, not your enemies. They are your colleagues; just the folks on the other side.[13] Actually, they are your only real friends in the courtroom, the only ones experiencing what you are experiencing, feeling what you are feeling, worrying about the same things you are worrying about. In my first trial, I couldn't figure out when it was my turn to challenge a juror prospect during the *voir dire*. The Prosecutor, whom I had just met, saw my confusion and helped me out with discrete nods of his head.

The process of trial is intense enough without letting it get personal. These are people whom you will probably see frequently. This trial ends, the next begins. Clients come and go, but adversaries remain. If you are going to be successful,[14]

---

[13] Yes, be kind. After all, life can't be easy for them – they have been burdened with the psyche of a prosecutor.

[14] I'm not sure what this means, by the way. My vulgar self measured success by wins. My professional self was generally happy if I did my job well, no matter the outcome. Actually, my professional self

you will need to be able to work with them as you work against them. I tried some very tough and heated cases against some very dear friends and feel fortunate they remained so. After a while, it all starts to feel like the gauntlet syndrome – "Whew, we survived that one. Are you OK? Guess we should get on to the next one." The physical "Bar" in the courtroom, the structure that separates the well of the arena from the public, is the metaphor and reality of your adversarial relationship. What happens on one side is not brought to the other.

It's also a good idea to make a conscious effort to know your adversaries. After all, they are your adversaries. They are an important part of the equation. They stand between you and what you want. Whether they are your best friend, a total stranger, or someone with whom you have an intense history, they have strengths and weaknesses and these values should always be part of your trial prep. Observe them. Who are you up against? Are they quick on their feet? Well-prepared? Savvy? Courtroom savvy?

---

is probably a lot larger and healthier in retrospect than it was back in the day. Then, I spent a lot of time in Al Davis mode – "Just win, baby!"

Outside of the courtroom, you will be negotiating a lot with your opponents. This is a crucial part of the process, since most of your cases will not go to trial but will end in a plea bargain. I regret that I didn't spend more time studying the art of negotiation. I totally recommend it. But I did learn that Kris Kristoferson had it right in *Me and Bobby MacGee*—"Freedom's just another word for nothing left to lose." Never leave your adversary with nothing to lose. You do not want an adversary who is "free" because there is nothing to gain by accepting your offer. What you are doing in this process is quantifying risk. Negotiation is not so much about what you have to gain, but what your adversary has to lose. Risk is the coin of the realm in the land of negotiation. If you focus on that element, you can spend it more wisely.

You do have one slight edge in negotiating with prosecutors. They carry the burden of the common weal. Not you. Your portfolio is to represent the defendant. Theirs' is to see justice done. There are occasions when you can appeal to their consciences, if they have one.

Respect your adversary, but not when they go "textile" on you. You know the government is on the run when they start to talk about "moral fiber". Or "fabric". Fiber and Fabric – sounds like a store in the garment district. But someday, I guarantee, a prosecutor will stand up and say that something your client is doing or has done will "rend the very[15] fabric of our society" or adversely affect its "moral fiber." I always laughed when this happened because it came to have the feeling of a cereal commercial:

> "Do you want to start your day with fiber?
> There is no higher fiber than moral fiber.
> ***Moral Fiber.***
> Breakfast of Prosecutors."

Of course, if you can only get those around you(a/k/a your spouse) to respect the process, then you can tell anyone who needs anything from you (call your mother-in-law, take out the garbage, etc.) that you cannot be disturbed because you are "on trial."   It's a wonderful excuse -- sort of the jurisprudential equivalent of "Not tonight, honey – I have a headache."

---

[15] "Very" is very important. It's never the fabric that gets rent; it's always the "very" fabric.

CONCLUSION

I hope that none of this sounds like carping. I am not disgruntled, but just a little weary from so many years of bucking the system. I certainly do not want to sour you. I would never want you to miss the sense of satisfaction when your pre-trial work comes to fruition in the courtroom, the delight when, out of the corner of your eye, you catch the jury perking up whenever you rise to do anything, the adrenalin rush at the moment you realize that you have gained control over an adverse witness, the unique excitement as you stare intensely at the throat, not the lips, of the foreperson announcing the verdict to see if the first sound to be formed is the voiced velar of the "G" in "Guilty" or the nasal "N" of "Not".

So, my best advice is to take it all seriously.

But, don't take it all SERIOUSLY.

The wins.

The losses.

In the great poker game of justice, they are not dealing you the good hands.

Obviously, these COMMANDMENTS are not

chiseled in marble and you will find yourself violating them over and over, hopefully out of desperation and not unawareness. Make friends with desperation. It will always be your companion and, if you play it right, the fuel that propels you on this exciting journey – if you make it so.